Animals
In The Zoo

by Feodor Rojankovsky

pinwheel books knopf/pantheon

FIRST PINWHEEL BOOKS EDITION—MARCH, 1973. Originally published by Alfred A. Knopf, Inc. in 1962. Copyright © 1962 by Feodor Rojankovsky. All rights reserved under International and Pan-American Copyright Conventions. Published in the United States by Random House, Inc., and simultaneously in Toronto, Canada, by Random House of Canada, Limited, Toronto. Manufactured in the United States of America. *Library of Congress Catalog Card Number:* 72-9564   ISBN 0-394-82622-1

B b Baboon

C c

Cheetah

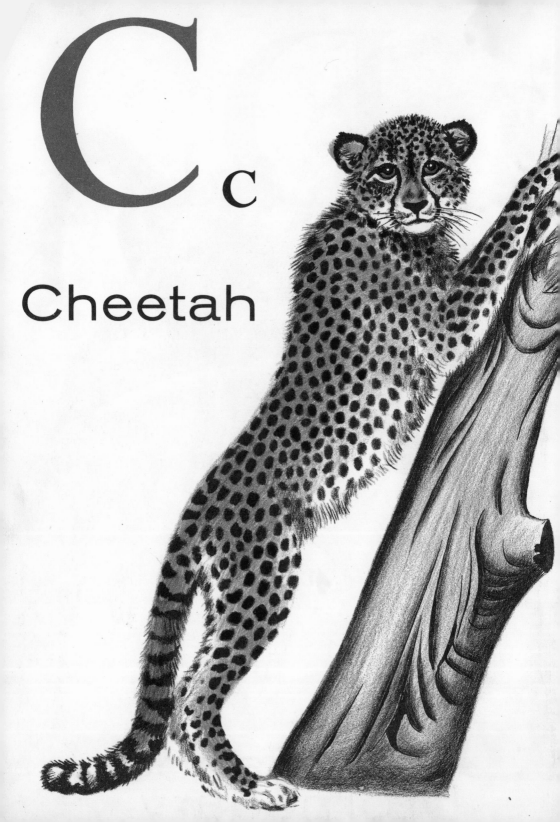

Dd

Dromedary

E e

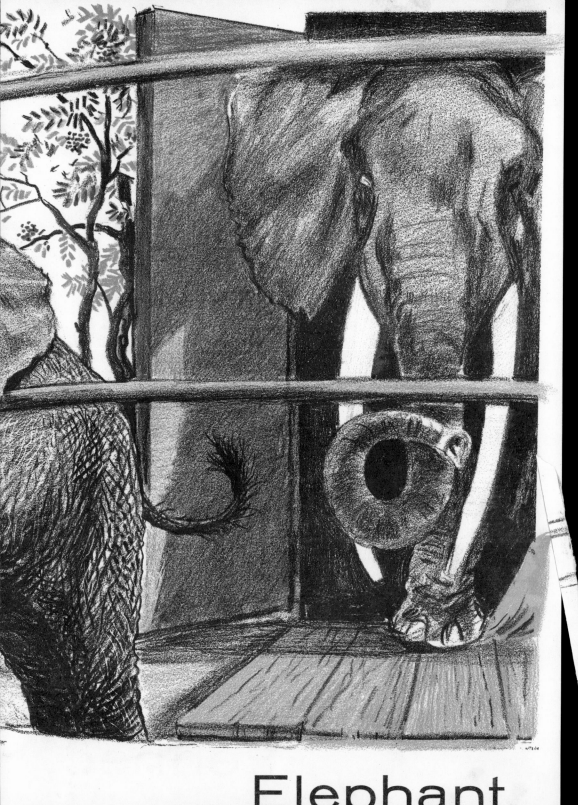

Elephant

F f

Fennec

G g

Giraffe

H h

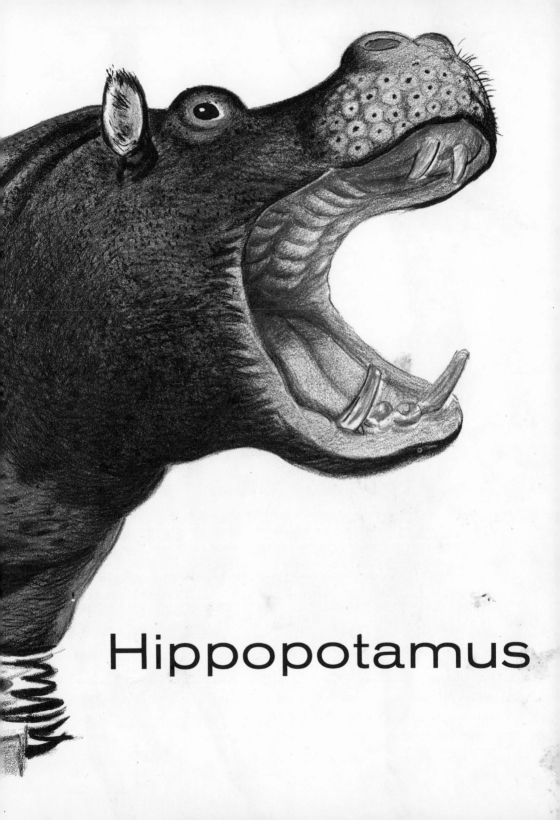

Hippopotamus

I i

Impa

J j

Jackrabbit

K k
Kangaroo

Lion

L l

M m

Mink

Nandu

N n

Owl

O o

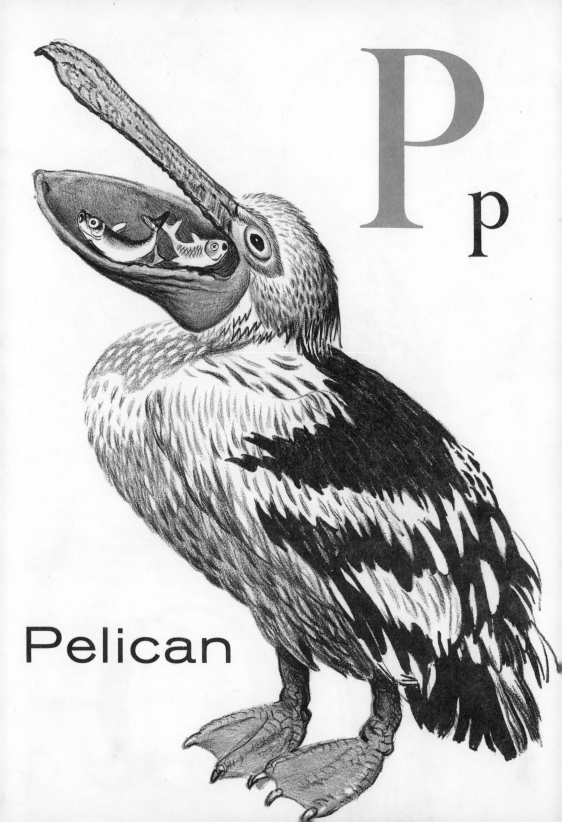

P p

Pelican

Quetzal

Q q

Reindeer

R r

S s

Seal

T t Tiger

U u

Urial

Vari

V
v

Wolf

W w

Xerus

X

x

Y y

Yak

Z z

Zebra

A B C D E F

G H I J K L

M N O P Q R

S T U V W X

Y Z